how to raise
show guppies

by lou wasserman

Cover photo by Rudolph Zukal.

Frontispiece by Dr. Herbert R. Axelrod.

ISBN 0-87666-453-2

Distributed in the U.S.A. by T.F.H. Publications, Inc., 211 West Sylvania Avenue, P.O. Box 27, Neptune City, N.J. 07753; in England by T.F.H. (Gt. Britain) Ltd., 13 Nutley Lane, Reigate, Surrey; in Canada to the book store and library trade by Clarke, Irwin & Company, Clarwin House, 791 St. Clair Avenue West, Toronto 10, Ontario; in Canada to the pet trade by Rolf C. Hagen Ltd., 3225 Sartelon Street, Montreal 382, Quebec; in Southeast Asia by Y.W. Ong, 9 Lorong 36 Geylang, Singapore 14; in Australia and the south Pacific by Pet Imports Pty. Ltd., P.O. Box 149, Brookvale 2100, N.S.W., Australia. Published by T.F.H. Publications Inc., Ltd., The British Crown Colony of Hong Kong.

Contents

DEDICATION

I dedicate this book to all those interested in raising guppies for show competition.

ACKNOWLEDGMENTS

I wish to express gratitude to the following:

Mr. Fred Samuelson, Brooklyn, N.Y.
who provided me with both good guppies and good advice when I was starting out and whose friendliness and patience have been a big help.

Mr. Ron Ahlers, formerly of Deer Park, N.Y. and now of West Palm Beach, Florida,
from whom I acquired my second set of quality breeding stock and through whom I gained advanced knowledge about guppy breeding.

Mrs. Midge Hill, Whittier, California,
whose articles about the international show circuit while she was Editor of *Guppy Roundtable* inspired me to participate.

Mr. Art Hopkins, Cincinnati, Ohio,
who, while president of the International Fancy Guppy Association, took valuable time and interest in teaching me to adjust to the show circuit. He taught me selection, packing and caring for my entries.

To Mr. Stan Shubel, Howell, Michigan,
a former president of the International Fancy Guppy Association, I wish to extend a special acknowledgment. In my opinion, this gentleman is the foremost authority in the world on the breeding, raising and showing of guppies. He has unselfishly volunteered information through articles, slide programs and tapes to further the knowledge of guppy breeding.

These wonderful people are among my most valued friends.

The Gratification of a Guppy Hobbyist

Breeding show guppies is a very rewarding hobby, one reason being that the production of guppies for entering into competition in guppy shows allows you to match your fish-raising skills with those of other people of like interest . . . and there is no more positive proof of the quality of your stock (and consequently no more positive proof of the degree of your skill) than to win with them in show competition.

The preparation involved in selecting forty to fifty top-quality guppies to enter in a show, the matching of tank entries, and the picking of spares in the event some of the guppies are unable to withstand the rigors of long-distance travel all require ability and experience. The average guppy fancier might be discouraged by the details involved in assuring success in the shipping of fish to the different show locations, which involves among other things factors like these: selection of the best air carrier to a particular show site, checking out departure and arrival times, considering the climatic conditions prevailing, etc. But if you enjoy a challenge, the International Fancy Guppy Association's show circuit can be well worth your time, effort and expense.

My guppies have been a complimentary reflection on my dedication and care whenever I've taken them to shows, and I come away from every show stimulated in my enthusiasm for really beautiful

The author with a few of his guppy awards. Photo by Phillip Schurch.

guppies. At least equally important, I am even more greatly stimulated and enriched at each show because of having been able to meet and exchange views with many people having the same interests I do. Make no mistake; the guppy-showing world numbers among it a share of weirdos and cranks and pests about equal to that found in the general population. But in the main guppy exhibitors are fun people; they're fun to be with, fun to know, fun to write to and hear from in the snowstorm of correspondence that many of us get involved with once we've begun to show guppies in earnest. I'm grateful to many of them for the things they've taught me and for having given me the opportunity to teach them things, too. If you get involved with showing guppies to the degree that I hope this book will enable you, you'll know exactly what I mean about the gratifications in store for you.

Right now I'm going to list my guppy-showing achievements to date, partly to show you what any novice guppy breeder can accomplish by sensibly applying his talents and partly to impress you with my qualifications so that you'll pay close attention to what I say in the rest of this book . . . it's good advice, and I hope you take it.

In shows held by the International Fancy Guppy Association during the seasons 1971 through part of 1976, I have won over 500 first place international trophies and almost 1600 awards (including more than 20 Best of Show awards). I have won world championships in the breeder male, half-black AOC, half-black red, half-black blue, half-black pastel, super widetail, blue and black classes. In addition, I have been three times (1971, 1973, 1974) named Guppy Man of the Year (the Guppy Man of the Year award is presented annually by Guppy Associates of Chicago to the participant accumulating the most "Best of Show" points throughout the season on the IFGA show circuit). Lastly—but far from least, since this award is considered to be the highest in the guppy field—I have twice (1973, 1974) won the World Champion Male Grand award.

Equipment

A fancier maintaining but one strain can do wonderfully well with six or eight tanks, preferably two 10-gallon tanks and six 15-gallon tanks.

Medium-sized tanks, about ten to twenty gallons in capacity, have proved to be the best to use; too small a tank inhibits the growth of the guppies, while too large a tank only limits the capacity of the normal aquarist to fit as many tanks as are necessary into the space available.

After meeting many guppy fanciers and studying their equipment, I tried to work out as efficient a guppy room as I could. This is the equipment I decided upon:

Tanks: Mostly 10-gallons. Bare-bottomed, plantless tanks are easier to care for.

Salt: I use one teaspoon of non-iodized salt for each gallon of aquarium water. My reason for using salt is two-fold: guppies like brackish water, and the live brine shrimp that I feed them will last longer with salt in the water.

Filters: Inside corner filters are inexpensive and easily cleaned and do the job efficiently. The filter material in each tank is changed every seven to ten days. I use marbles in my filters to keep the filters weighted down. I don't use charcoal, just filter wool . . . but remember that you have to change the filter material often, and you have to make water changes often.

Siphon Hose: I use a 5/8'' siphon hose to remove the fish waste and uneaten food from the bottom of

There are many different shapes and sizes of inside corner filters on the market, and all are suitable for use in tanks housing guppies. They have the advantage of being economical and taking up little room as well as being easy to service.

the aquarium daily. This results in about a 10% water change per day.

Spawning Grass: Unless a mature guppy is so stuffed with food that it cannot hold any more, it will eat baby guppies. For this reason it has become the custom to use breeding traps in which the female is confined while the young may escape before being eaten. I do not feel that this is a good idea. First, the mother should not be cooped up in so small a space; secondly, it is very difficult to control the food, since most of it falls through the trap. I much prefer to use spawning grass which holds back the mothers but not the babies.

Pumps: The air pumps you use will mostly depend on how many tanks you have and to a smaller degree what type of filtration system you use. The more tanks you have, the more powerful the pump you'll need. The more air your filters require, the more you'll have to provide. I think that a small-scale breeder with just half a dozen or so tanks can get by with a good vibrator pump or two; he can use a piston pump if he wants to, of course, and making an investment in a good piston pump will allow him to expand his air production as he acquires more tanks, but he shouldn't need a piston pump to begin with.

Heaters: I live in Florida and therefore don't have to be as concerned with winter weather as guppy people living in more northerly areas, but even here we have cold snaps. I have too many tanks to heat each tank with its own individual

The author uses artificial spawning grass rather than live plants or breeding traps to save baby guppies from their mother. Here a floating mop of artificial spawning grass is shown being used in a plastic nursery tank. The many babies already delivered can find refuge from their mother (who is due to drop many more fry) by swimming up into the grass. Photo by Phillip Schurch.

A siphoning device of some type is an inexpensive but indispensable part of every guppy breeder's equipment.

Whether you use an older style floating or hanging thermometer or one of the newer digital thermometers, you need an accurate temperature gauge, because provision of the correct temperature is very important to guppies' development and continued good health.

heater, and many other large-scale producers are in the same position. Instead of heating each individual tank, we heat the entire room housing the tanks. Now heating a room for long periods to the temperature at which guppies do best (80° F. in my opinion) can be an expensive proposition. In some cases, depending mostly on where the guppy tanks are situated within the home, it might not even be within the range of the achievable. So even a guppy breeder having the minimum breeding set-up of six

The type of pump used (vibrator type shown here) depends primarily on how many tanks have to be serviced. Obviously, the greater the number of tanks, the more powerful the air supply would have to be. Some guppy breeders favor the use of piston pumps over vibrator pumps as they acquire more tanks, since the piston pumps generally are more powerful, but others simply add new vibrator pumps to handle the increased number of tanks. Really large-scale breeders sometimes use air compressors.

or eight tanks should try to place his tanks in a room within the home that will be heated as a normal part of the home atmosphere and won't require heating just to keep the guppies happy; if the room is kept warm enough for human comfort, a heater in each tank will be able to raise the temperature into the guppy-comfort area without costing too much in electrical consumption. In other words, when you're setting up your breeding establishment, make sure you take temperature into consideration, and obtain whatever heating apparatus you need. A chilled guppy is a sick guppy, and a really cold guppy will soon be a dead guppy.

Lighting Equipment: If you have many tanks and a separate fish room for them, you're better off with a single powerful light source than with an individual reflector on each tank. Even a comparatively small set-up holding six or eight tanks can be lighted more economically from one central source than by individual reflectors.

Water

Guppies should never be put into an aquarium containing totally new water. At least 50% of a new set-up should be water taken from an aquarium in which guppies have been living. I remember from past experience that when I had introduced guppies into brand new water, they either hung at the top of the tank or hovered at the bottom. It sometimes took as long as a week before they began to act normally. Now when I set up a new tank I use 50% raw tap water treated to remove chlorine and 50% old guppy water.

When transferring guppies from one tank to another, whether it be within your own fish room or from a completely different area, the fish should be put into water that has approximately the same acidity/alkalinity and hardness qualities as the original water from which they came. Every effort should be made to come as close as possible to the original water whether it was 6.8 acid water, 8.3 alkaline water, 17-35 ppm soft water or 240-260 ppm hard water.

It is important to replace **at least** 20% of the aquarium water every week. I prefer to siphon off 10% of the water every day. I feel this is the most important reason for my rapid rise to the top of the guppy world.

I started siphoning every day after reading an article by Fred Grimm which appeared in *Guppy Roundtable*. It told how the author's wife had secretly experimented with one of his tanks of show-quality half-black reds. He began to notice that in one particular tank the males were turning out to be far superior to any he had previously raised. After these fish had taken a Best in Show, his wife admitted that she had siphoned that tank every day.

That article started me on my program of daily water changes of smaller amounts of water instead of the more usual custom of changing larger amounts less often. Not only has this paid off in bigger and better fish, but it also averted what could have been a major disaster.

The day that I could have lost all my guppies started like any other normal day. I fed my 7:30 A.M. feeding and siphoned my 175 aquariums. As I started replacing the water I had siphoned out with raw tap water I began to notice that in some of the tanks the guppies seemed to be bunching up at the top and just hanging. In other tanks they cowered on the bottom. Obviously, something was very wrong, and the only thing my panic-stricken mind could come up with was that it was being caused by a chlorine build-up. I quickly poured SuperChlor into all my tanks. Almost instantly the fish began to act more normally, with the exception of one 15-gallon tank from which I had siphoned two gallons instead of the usual one and a half gallons. In this tank all the males' tails began to disintegrate.

I called the water company and learned that they had put an excess amount of chlorine into the water because of a bacteria build-up. Instead of the normal 1.0-1.5 parts per million of chlorine, the water was coming out with a reading of 2.0-2.5 ppm chlorine.

In order to avoid such dangers in the future I decided to get more information by visiting the water company. I took along a sample of my own water. Only two months before my water had tested

Water hardness and pH test kits are available at pet shops everywhere and can be acquired at comparatively little expense, as can products used to dechlorinate water. Hobbyists considering the breeding of guppies on a serious basis should have their own water-testing equipment so that they can check water quality at any time.

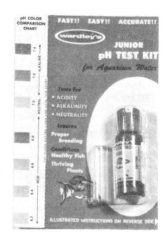

out as pH 7.4, with a hardness of about 225 ppm. To my amazement it tested out this time as pH 8.3 and hardness 156 ppm. I asked the water company how this was possible, and they showed me their weekly testing chart, which is taken at six-hour intervals. Here is a sample of what they showed me:

1st day:

pH readings:	7.7	8.0	8.5	8.7
Hardness:	100 ppm	96 ppm	96 ppm	80 ppm

2nd day:

pH readings:	8.0	8.1	7.0	7.1
Hardness:	280 ppm	260 ppm	252 ppm	272 ppm

3rd day:

pH readings:	8.9	9.1	9.3	8.8
Hardness:	84 ppm	78 ppm	152 ppm	140 ppm

This might explain why the fish behave strangely after having been subjected to a large change of water. Can you imagine changing 40% of the aquarium water with a pH reading of 7.1 and hardness of 156 ppm and assuming that the tap water is the same when actually the reading for that particular time might be pH 9.1 and hardness 78 ppm?

I can only sum this up by advising you to change small amounts often and check with your local water company.

Feeding

There is an old saying among guppy people that "guppies are what they eat." I have always assumed that the saying means that—granting a certain level of potential development resulting from the fish's genetic material—good feeding produces good guppies and bad feeding produces bad guppies. At the very least, I think, it means that good feeding produces better guppies than bad feeding produces, and it means also that a good guppy will be better if fed well than if not fed well. (It also would mean that a bad guppy will be a worse guppy if not fed well, but we're not really concerned with developing that theme.)

From various of the publications that I have read, I'm sure that there are people around who know an awful lot about guppy nutrition. They can tell you which vitamins guppies need and which they don't need, the exact effects of hormones used in guppies' foods, the exact rate of growth of guppies maintained on a diet of tubifex worms or brine shrimp as opposed to the exact rate of growth of guppies maintained on a diet of chopped rubber bands. They know these things because they have a good scientific background in fish nutrition and biochemistry, and they have conducted exhaustive experimentation to get answers to questions about nutrition. Unfortunately for you (or perhaps fortunately—it all depends on how you look at it), I am not a fish nutritionist. I can't and won't tell you which vitamins a guppy needs; I can tell you only what has worked for me on the basis of long experience, and I can spell that out in just a few short words: feed a varied diet, and feed often.

The foods I use are foods that are available to you. I have no secret formulas and use no home-made concoctions; I use a combination of live foods and commercial fish foods, the same brands of fish foods that are sold in pet shops all over the country. I feed live baby brine shrimp twice a day (at 11:30 in the morning and 10:30 at night), and I feed dry commercial foods six times a day (7:30 A.M., 9:30 A.M., 2:30 P.M., 4:30 P.M., 6:30 P.M., 8:30 P.M.), with one of three paste foods every day at 11:00 A.M. The commercial prepared foods that I use in my feeding program were chosen because of their different ingredients. I don't just select a bundle of different brands and hope that they will provide enough of a variety; I choose among the different brands for their specific differences. One food may be high in vegetable content, another high in meat content; one may be high in fish content, another high in trace elements and vitamins. I am listing here the actual brands that I use. As time goes by and new foods come out, you can be sure that I'll be experimenting with them to see whether they can help me breed better, bigger guppies. The foods that I'm currently feeding to my fish are: Tetra FD 4-in-1 (for its high meat content); Aquatrol Salmon Flakes and Squid Flakes (for their high fish and marine animal contents); Tetra Conditioning Food (for good vegetable content); Results Flake Food and Kordon Diet 15 (for cereals plus vitamins and trace elements); Tops (because of its high protein and good variety of ingredients); Rut-King because it's an old favorite; Wardley's Guppy Flakes because they're made specifically for guppies and Peekskill (the paste food). By choosing different

There are two main features in any good guppy feeding program: feed very often and feed a great variety of foods so that as many *different* nutritional needs as possible can be covered. It is not enough to simply pick out a variety of different brands; you also have to check the contents of the brands so that you can choose different sources of nutrition. There is no sense, for example, in just picking out four different brands of processed brine shrimp and thinking that you are thereby providing a balanced diet. Luckily for guppy breeders, both beginning and experienced, the aquarium market offers a very wide variety of food formulations and food-enrichment additives in the form of vitamins and minerals, and new foods are coming onto the market all the time.

foods from different makers on the basis of the foods' contents and claims I'm assured of a wide range of different nutritive elements, and I can more or less touch all nutritional bases. What one maker's product lacks, another's might supply. The people who make the foods know more about nutrition than I do, so I might as well take advantage of their expertise and the research they've done.

The major reason why many guppy fanciers fail to raise guppies to their best is that they simply do not feed often enough. They don't scrimp and try to save on ingredients—they buy the best they can, in fact—but they just don't feed *enough*. This is a big mistake, because a guppy's digestive tract fills and empties in a comparatively short time. Any healthy guppy will eat ten times a day; if you don't provide food for him to eat ten times a day, you're short-changing him and of course coincidentally short-changing yourself of the enjoyment really good guppies can provide, regardless of how much you pay for your foods. My theory about keeping food in front of my guppies all day long accounts for my use of paste foods, by the way. They have the advantage of being able to remain in the aquarium for a relatively long period without fouling the water, and this allows the guppies to nibble at them during the day. If any of the paste food remains uneaten until the following morning, it is removed when I siphon (which I do every day).

I don't make any distinction between the commercial foods I feed baby guppies and what I feed adults; all are fed the same varieties and with the same frequency.

I feel that the live baby brine shrimp I feed my guppies twice a day are the single most important element in their feeding program. Live baby brine shrimp are eaten with gusto by both baby guppies and adult guppies, and one of the biggest advantages of using brine shrimp nauplii is that the nauplii last in the aquarium for quite some time, so you can feed generously only twice a day and still have a sufficient number remain in the tank for the guppies to pick on as the mood strikes them. Based on my own long experiences in raising good guppies, I can say with certainty that there is a tremendous difference between the amount of growth put on by baby guppies fed exclusively on dry foods and the growth put on by baby guppies fed a mixture of dry foods and live baby brine shrimp. Guppies fed on the latter diet outstrip in every respect the fish fed on the diet of dry foods exclusively. For those readers who don't know how to make good use of brine shrimp eggs to hatch out live baby shrimp, here is my method; perhaps you can put it to good use.

HATCHING BRINE SHRIMP

The following hatching instructions are for hatching the San Francisco brine shrimp eggs, which are the only ones I use. The newly hatched brine shrimp are the most nutritious. The longer they are held, the less benefit your guppies derive.

I find the large size IV (intravenous) bottle excellent for hatching this beneficial food. The first tube is a flexible airline tubing to inject air. The second is a rigid tube which extends just above the water level to allow the air to return to the outside. This adaptation of an IV bottle prevents the water from splashing all over everything.

I use 8 tablespoons of Kosher salt to one gallon of water (Kosher salt is free of additives). This should give a hydrometer reading of 1.020. At a room temperature of 80 degrees, which I consider

Right: An intravenous bottle used by the author to hatch brine shrimp in quantity. As can be seen, the water is being heavily aerated, creating agitation of the brine mixture containing the eggs. **Below:** An adult female brine shrimp surrounded by newly hatched brine shrimp nauplii. Photo by Dr. C.W. Emmens.

The difference in the size of guppies raised by different breeders is caused mostly by the breeders' different feeding practices, and this holds true even on an international level. Guppies produced by European breeders generally lack the size of guppies produced by American breeders, even though European guppies such as the German-bred specimen shown above often excel in color and fin shape. Guppies from the Far East, on the other hand, usually show very good size but are less distinguished in color and regularity of finnage. (The guppy shown below was bred by Ong Ban Choon in Singapore.) Upper photo by Dr. Karl Knaack.

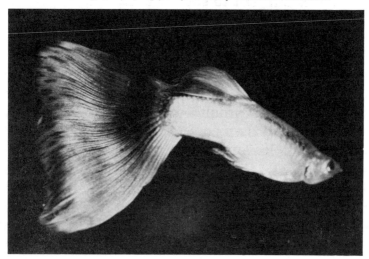

ideal, I start the hatch and allow 36 hours hatching time. For the large number of guppies and the frequency with which I feed, it is necessary for me to rotate three IV bottles at a time to make sure all my guppies can be fed an adequate supply according to the schedule.

At feeding time I shut off the air supply fifteen minutes before harvesting the shrimp. This allows the live shrimp to sink to the bottom and the unhatched eggs and shells to rise to the top. I then take the tube off the air valve and drop the end of the tube into a fine net which drains into a receptacle. The net full of shrimp is rinsed in clear water and squeezed slightly to eliminate as much salt water as possible to prevent additional salt from entering the aquariums. When all the live brine shrimp have been used, I drain the jar, rinse it thoroughly and set up with a fresh hatch.

It is important to store the brine shrimp eggs in their original container at room temperature so that they remain completely dry.

Unfortunately, the supply of brine shrimp eggs right now is subject to such a great degree of variance in quantity (you sometimes can't get them at all) and quality (if you get them they might hatch out very poorly) that you might have to make at least temporary substitutions of other live foods for the brine shrimp. I've experimented with various other live foods common in the aquarium hobby and have come to my own conclusions about them, and I list those conclusions in the following paragraphs. The main thing to remember is that although none of the other foods is better than live baby brine shrimp, they all are better than no live food at all. The big advantage of live foods, apart from whatever superiority they might have over prepared

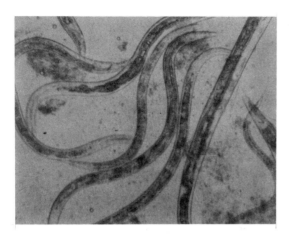

Species of nematode worms like the *Turbatrix* species shown here are often marketed as food for baby guppies. Photo by Helmert.

commercial foods just by virtue of their being alive instead of processed, is that they stay alive in the tank at least for a while and therefore allow the fish to take food as they choose. In this regard they are of course superior to frozen baby brine shrimp, although frozen baby brine shrimp is an excellent food and comes pretty close to the live brine shrimp in food value.

Two of the foods (microworms and micro-eels) are mostly used to feed baby guppies, although the adult fish will eat them too, and two of the foods (fruitflies and white worms) are used for adult guppies. There are many other suitable live foods and many other methods of culturing the foods discussed, and I suggest that if you want to pursue the subject you refer to some of the live food books that are on the market; they'll give you some very good ideas. Two books that I recommend are *Live Foods for the Aquarium and Terrarium* by Willy Jocher and the *Encyclopedia of Live Foods* by Charles O. Masters; both are published by T.F.H. Publications and are available at pet shops and book stores.

Microworms: The best brine shrimp substitute, in my opinion. To set up your microworm cultures, put *yellow* cornmeal to a depth of half an inch in the bottom of a plastic container (I use a plastic shoe box). In a separate container, mix dry yeast in water until a slightly milky solution results, then wet the cornmeal with the yeast-water mixture leaving a small puddle or two; then add a few drops of the microworm culture. Make at least two more cultures in the same way to keep a supply going. If a smell develops in the cultures, add a pinch of yeast to provide a "baking bread" aroma. Each culture will last more than two months if more cornmeal and yeast-water are added each week.

Micro-eels: Using a glass container that holds no

A microworm culture maintained in a plastic dish. Photo by Robert Gannon.

more than four to six ounces of water, add half a pinch of yellow cornmeal and one pinch of sugar to each ounce of water, then add about a teaspoonful (in total, not per ounce) of micro-eels to seed the culture. Keep scum from forming at the top of the culture or the worms (which is indeed what the "eels" are) will die quickly.

A culture should be ready for harvesting in about a week. To feed, simply pour some of the culture through a very fine-mesh net and then swish the net through the aquarium, then pour the strained fluid back into the micro-eel culture. Micro-eel cultures have the nasty habit of getting smelly, so you'll have to experiment a little bit to see what works best for you to control odors.

Wingless Fruitflies. Add yellow cornmeal to a depth of a quarter of an inch in the bottom of a bottle. Mix a little dry yeast in water until the solution becomes milky, then dampen the cornmeal thoroughly with the yeast-water solution, but don't leave any puddles. Add at least seven flies to the bottle and cover it with a cover into which you've punched at least one tiny nail hole; lay a paper towel over the top of the bottle before you screw on the nail-punched cover. To harvest the flies for feeding, tap the culture bottle; the flies will fall to the bottom and can then be shaken out into the aquarium. After you have some experience with culturing fruitflies you might want to graduate to using agar cultures.

White Worms. White worms are enchytraeid worms that can be raised by the thousands in just a few days. Raise the worms in soil and feed them cooked oatmeal, bread or cereal twice a week. Keep the culture just damp, not saturated, and cover the food with a little soil to prevent the formation of mold; the worms will gather around the food.

A cluster of white worms just after being removed from their culture medium. Photo by Robert Gannon.

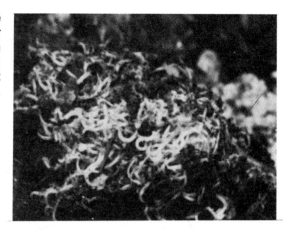

Fruit flies. The flies shown are not the vestigial-winged form that should be used by hobbyists for live food cultures, although they are the same species, *Drosophila melanogaster.* Photo by Paul Imgrund.

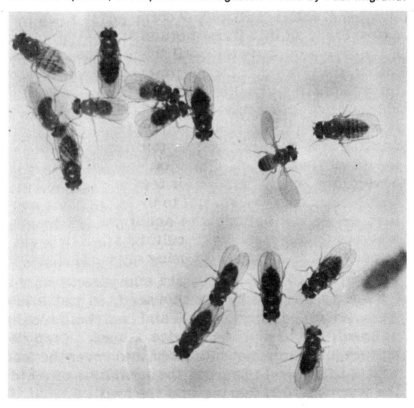

A Typical Day

My guppy room is a 15 foot x 15 foot addition on my home. It houses 175 aquariums ranging in size from 10 gallons to 80 gallons in capacity. Already I feel a serious need for more space.

The room is illuminated by four 8-foot fluorescent lights controlled automatically. The first two go on at 7:00 A.M., followed fifteen minutes later by the other two. The lights are staggered so that the fish slowly become accustomed to the bright light.

7:30 A.M. — Feeding - dried food.

8:00 A.M. — Siphon 10% of the water from the bottom of each tank. Replace an equal amount directly from the tap. Add 1 teaspoon of pure Kosher salt. Because I have such a large operation I run my tap water through a carbon filter which removes the chlorine instantly. For the average guppy raiser I would suggest adding a chlorine remover.

9:30 A.M. — Feeding - dried food.

10:00 A.M. — Change filters. I change filters in a percentage of my tanks every day. I remove the filters from the next fifteen or so tanks to be cleaned. Clean filters are taken from the bleach water in which they have been soaking all night, rinsed thoroughly, weighted with marbles, packed with filter floss and put into the tanks whose filters I had removed. The dirty filters are rinsed and put to soak overnight in the bleach water. I do not have to bother with charcoal, since I do not need it because of my daily siphoning schedule. However, charcoal is an ideal method of purifying aquarium water and one I recommend for the hobbyist with a smaller

Doing the work involved with maintaining guppy tanks in good condition is a time-consuming chore for hobbyists who intend to raise guppies on a large scale, but the work must be done regularly and conscientiously. Photo by Phillip Schurch.

operation. If you use charcoal I suggest you frequently rinse it thoroughly, spread it out on a clean paper and place it in the sun to dry, making sure to turn it occasionally.

11:00 A.M. — Feeding - paste food.

11:30 A.M. — Feeding - live brine shrimp.

 2:30 P.M. — Feeding - dry food.

 4:30 P.M. — Feeding - dry food.

 6:30 P.M. — Feeding - dry food.

 8:30 P.M. — Feeding - dry food.

10:30 P.M. — Feeding - live brine shrimp.

 1:00 A.M. — The first two fluorescents go off, followed fifteen minutes later by the other two.

I am constantly separating males from. females, culling, setting up breeders, packing guppies, shipping guppies, etc. With this busy schedule, my family and I still find time to enjoy the beach.

Selection of Breeding Stock

After food and environment the most important factor in maintaining good guppies is the selection of breeding stock.

There is absolutely no question of leaving males and females to breed together in a single batch. Everything will go wrong. The quicker, smaller and more runty males will beat the better ones and the result will be a rapid deterioration of the stock, even though the strain had previously been brought to a relatively perfect state.

It is best to breed the selected young guppies in small communities rather than in individual pairs or in larger communities. Two males to five females in a 10-gallon aquarium will form a very useful breeding nucleus.

Use only the best young males. A word of caution: do not wait until the males are fully matured and in their prime to introduce them to the females. Old, fully-developed males are not always fertile or able to complete the sexual act efficiently.

I select my males at three to five months of age, depending on their growth. The half-black pastels are slower growing, so I select them at about five months. The half-black reds and black orchids can be selected at four months. The reds, blues, greens, purples and snakeskins are my most rapid growers and may be selected at three months.

More often than not the average guppy breeder, when selecting his breeding stock, will leave the best males in the tank. He usually selects the biggest, flashiest males . . . the ones that stand out

A group of magnificent half-black red males showing excellent uniformity. These fish were only 2½ months old when photographed, but they have the potential to carry on in the winning tradition of their ancestors, which have won the IFGA world half-black red championship for four years in a row. Photo by Dr. Herbert R. Axelrod of fish bred by the author.

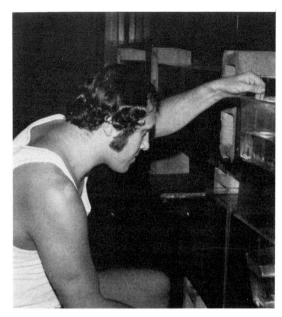

The author checking a guppy during the culling process. The fish is held in the net and glven individual inspection for good points and bad points. Photo by Phillip Schurch.

A male from William Illig's blue snakeskin strain; guppies like this can result only from the application of knowledge and attention to detail.

among the rest . . . without regard to any imperfections they might have.

When I select my male breeders I remove all the males to a 1½-gallon rectangular aquarium, making it easier to see any imperfections. First I look for body size, eliminating all thin-bodied males who will be unable to carry the weight of a wide tail as they mature. Also, the larger the body, the larger the tail is likely to be. Then I look for the most desired caudal, which is triangular-shaped and tapered. All other caudal shapes are eliminated. I then look at the color of the dorsal, always trying to match the dorsal color closely with the color of the caudal.

Now I go back to the caudal. Looking closely at the color, I eliminate all off-color fish. Then I weed out any fish with flat heads or ridges between the eyes. What I have left is my breeding and future show stock.

The females can be bred at about two months if they have been properly raised and fed. This makes the most of their potential for the production of young, as they will begin to decline in fertility after the age of eight or ten months. At the age of six to eight weeks the females with the best body formation are selected for breeders.

It is important to breed the females as early as six to eight weeks because, in my opinion, females kept without males will lose female hormones with age. It has been my experience that the longer they are kept virgin, the less fertile they become. They will gain in size and increase in radiance, but lose in fertility.

The gestation period is from 21 to 45 days, depending on the temperature of the water. I maintain a temperature of approximately 80 degrees, and my

Except for its big body this multicolored guppy doesn't have anything going for it. Its dorsal fin is much too small, and its caudal is terrible in shape. Photo by Victor Datzkevich.

This is a good yellow bicolor snakeskin with an especially pleasing color pattern in the tail. The dorsal is not large, but snakeskins are not noted for long dorsals. Photo by Victor Datzkevich.

You can't apply all of the same criteria that you use for culling male guppies to female guppies, of course, but the quality of your female breeders must be maintained with the same diligence as used for the males. This excellent female was bred in Germany. Photo by Dr. Karl Knaack.

guppies spawn roughly every 28 to 30 days.

Each strain has different breeding capabilities depending, in part, on how long the guppies have been inbred.

Maintaining a Strain

I am not interested in breeding guppies by the methods used by others. Many breeders are inclined to rely too heavily on their knowledge of biology and laws of inheritance and the theories that are used to chart the possible ways that certain characteristics can be inherited; I believe that "guppy genes" are too variable to be charted—or at least they're too variable for me to chart. I feel that these things have helped in many fields, but not in guppy breeding.

There are many ways that one can breed guppies. To list a few: in-breeding, line-breeding, out-crossing, and harem-breeding.

In-breeding is the mating of a pair of guppies that are closely (that is, being no farther removed in consanguinity than first cousins) related to one another. Examples are parent to offspring, brother to sister, first cousin to first cousin.

Line-breeding is the mating of guppies having common but fairly distant relatives such as grandparents or great-grandparents.

Out-crossing is the mating of guppies of two distantly related lines.

Harem-breeding is allowing guppies to breed together indiscriminately in a single batch. In my opinion, this is the worst method of breeding guppies. It will always be the smallest males that mate with the females.

Here is what I do in my method of breeding guppies. First of all, I acquire the finest stock I'm able to afford. Let's call this trio Parental Group #1. After the females in Parental Group #1 have produced

Two nearly perfectly matched black deltatails. Their only fault is that their dorsals are much too light. Photo by Midge Hill of fish bred by J. and J. Parrott. Fish of the Parrotts' strain won the IFGA Black Class championship for 1972 and 1973.

This blue veiltail shows good potential with its nicely matched dorsal and caudal, good body shape and nice caudal color. Photo by Dr. Herbert R. Axelrod.

A multicolor with a large body and caudal fin and a very tiny dorsal. This fish would not get a second look at an IFGA show. Photo by Victor Datzkevich.

young, I select the largest females in the fry group and breed them back to their father (the male in Parental Group #1. If the father is still sexually active by the time females produced by Parental Group #2 have matured, I breed him to them; if he's not, I breed the females to one of the males produced by Parental Group #1. These females and their father (or other male) make up Parental Group #3.

For parental Group #4 I use older brother to younger sister matings, January's males to March's females, for example. The reason for this I will explain by recounting an experience I had about ten years ago, around the time I first became seriously interested in breeding guppies. It was at this time I acquired my first outstanding breeding stock, a trio of half-black reds from a well-known New York guppy breeder. When the babies from the trio were a month old I removed six females to insure their virginity. When the males were developed I selected what I considered to be the best young males and attempted to breed them to their sisters. Two, then three months went by, but none of the females had any young. I was then forced to use the harem-females' babies (the females that I had left with their brothers). For the next two years I continued to attempt to breed selected males to their sisters, to no avail. Because of the continued harem-breeding, my strain of guppies had deteriorated. At this time I contacted the original breeder and explained to him what had taken place. I told him that I couldn't understand why the females that I removed to breed with their brothers never got pregnant, but the harem-females did. He explained to me that female guppies have a membrane, a soft layer of tissue that covers the vent, and that in certain strains of guppies, the one I was working with in particular, the longer she is kept virgin the thicker the membrane becomes. By the time my males were developed, my females' membranes had become so thick the males could not penetrate it. This explanation surely seemed logical at the time, so for the next three years I told everybody about the membrane on the female guppy. When I started on the international show circuit though, I discovered that the breeder was wrong, that the female guppy doesn't have a membrane. I now believe that the longer a female is kept virgin the less fertile she becomes because she is losing female hormones with age. This is why I breed my females at 6-8 weeks.

As the cycles are completed and my strains improving for approximately seven generations, I find it necessary to breed to a related strain with what I call a double-cross. I take males from line "A" and breed them with females from line "B," at the same time reversing this procedure and breeding males from line "B" with females from line "A." The males selected at this time are between three and five months old, depending on the strain—young enough to allow me to breed them to their daughters, but developed enough for me to decide whether or not they have the characteristics I'm looking for. After this cycle is complete (six to eight generations) I feel it's time to introduce a new male or female from another breeder who has an in-bred strain that closely resembles mine but is not related. My goal is to acquire stock that has desirable traits that mine lack. For instance, my strain of blue guppies has a short dorsal and could use a bigger body. I then look for a strain that has a large dorsal and a big body. By mixing the best of the two strains together the results should be an improvement.

One of the first winning half-black reds in the world, produced by Fred Samuelson in the early 1960's. Photo by S. Gollub.

The author uses half-black red gold males like the one shown here to breed into his line of half-black reds to keep good red color in the caudal. Photo by Dr. Herbert R. Axelrod.

This half-black blue comes from a strain that has won the world championship for half-black blues four years in a row. Fish in the strain are known for their large size and the good color match between dorsal and caudal. Photo by Dr. Herbert R. Axelrod of fish bred by the author.

Preparation for Showing

Preparation for showing begins the day my guppies are born. The first six weeks of feeding will make or break a show guppy. At the age of four weeks I remove all females from aquariums housing males that have been designated for showing. There are several reasons for this: the females grow bigger, take up space and eat more, and the males are constantly chasing after them. My show tanks are culled more ruthlessly than those tanks in which I raise guppies to sell.

At three months of age only ten to twelve males are kept in a 10-gallon aquarium so that they are not crowded. Males require a large amount of room for rapid growth and proper development.

Vitamins: At five months I begin using Vitamin B-12. I add 1 cc of water soluble B-12 (each cc contains 1000 mcg.) for every 10 gallons of water, every week. My black guppies are very susceptible to tail splitting, so I use 2 cc's per 10 gallons of water twice a week. Two weeks prior to show time I increase the usage of B-12 to every other day.

Trimming Guppies: Although I do not trim the caudal fins of my show guppies, many breeders do. If you have a guppy that you would like to show but it has a ragged caudal fin, you can carefully trim that part off and show the guppy. Always wet your hands when handling a guppy. Make sure to wet the platform where you will place the guppy. Lay the guppy down gently and use a brand new razor blade to cut with, as you need a very sharp blade. Place the blade at a slight angle and cut straight down.

Don't use a sawing action . . . just cut down and away. Trim off as little as possible, because a guppy with a large caudal has a better chance of winning than one with a smaller caudal.

Now, pick up the guppy gently with your hand so that you have access to the wound. Spread the caudal fin and paint it with a 2% solution of Mercurochrome. Make sure that no Mercurochrome gets into the guppy's gills, as it can cause damage to them. As an extra precaution you could re-paint the caudal fin in two days.

Enhancing Guppy Color: Many breeders of show guppies use special foods just before show time for the purpose of enhancing the color. Black guppies, for example, can be made blacker by feeding them prepared foods that contain additives that bring out the black color. Foods like this should not be fed all the time, however, but only in small quantities twice a day just prior to a show (starting no more than a week before show time).

Final Preparations: I stop all feeding at least 24 hours prior to shipping. This decreases the contamination of the shipping water from guppy waste and uneaten foods. Adult guppies are not harmed by missing a few days of feeding. My show guppies get their last feeding on a Wednesday night and are not fed again until the following Monday night.

Judged by IFGA show standards, this multicolor male is a very poor specimen. If your strain looks like this, you'd be better off starting all over with different fish.

These red bicolor guppies have exceptional tail color but nothing else to recommend them. Photo by H. Hansen, Aquarium Berlin.

This half-black male is typical of many German guppies, very brightly colored but usually on the small side. Photo by G. Gellrich.

The Show Itself

When your fish have been received by the member responsible for shipped-in fish at the show, they will be taken either to his house or directly to the show for benching, depending on how long before the show they have arrived.

During benching the shipping container is opened. The guppies, along with the water they were shipped in, are carefully poured into half-gallon drum bowls. They are then registered, labeled and put on the show bench.

Normally benching takes place on Saturday and judging begins on Sunday morning. When judging is taking place you may be allowed to follow along, and often you are permitted to ask questions about why a particular entry is either chosen or disqualified.

After the judging is over, the show is open to the public for viewing. An auction often follows the award presentation. I normally do not permit my guppies to be auctioned, but some participants do. The rare exceptions to my attitude are the California or Chicago shows, because the guppies usually command a higher price at shows in those areas. Normal practice is that 25% of the auction sale price is retained by the club hosting the show.

After the show your guppies are carefully packed into the fresh bags you should have included with your shipment and repacked into the shipping container, which is then taken to the airport for the journey home.

Guppy shows attract entrants and spectators of all ages and a wide diversity of occupations. . . young and old, wealthy and not-so-wealthy, male and female, they all have just one characteristic in common: a love for good guppies. Here contestants at a show are lining up to get bowl numbers for entering their fish. Photo by Midge Hill.

There are usually from ten to twelve shows per year sanctioned by the International Fancy Guppy Association in various parts of the country. Three of these shows are accompanied by important I.F.G.A. meetings. These are the three shows which I try to attend personally. The meeting and banquet are generally held on Saturday and Saturday night of the show week-end and are attended by all the guppy people you usually only read about. These experts are friendly and free with their knowledge, and the bull sessions are often the highlight of the show.

This is a very good blue male. The fish has large body size and a large caudal, and the color in the caudal is good except for a few minor red spots. The fish has a fault, though: the dorsal is too small and too light in color. Photo by Midge Hill of fish bred by Dale Marteeny.

Purple is a delicate color and difficult to capture photographically, so this photo unfortunately can't do justice to the subtleties of the guppy's coloration, but this is a good fish. The dorsal and caudal match very well. The ragged tail came from chasing too many females. Photo by Dr. Herbert R. Axelrod.

This multicolored male has a big body, but its small dorsal doesn't match the poorly shaped big tail. Photo by Victor Datzkevich.

AFTER THE SHOW

When the guppies arrive home from the show I check them over carefully. They are then put into a separate aquarium and isolated from my other guppies. As a preventive medication against protozoan disease I treat these aquariums with formaldehyde, adding two drops per gallon, and tetracycline (250 mg.), 1 capsule for each 5 gallons of water.

I have lost more show guppies to protozoan disease than anything else. The disease appears as a red line at the edge of the tail, and in some cases the tail begins to close up. This disease is highly contagious and must be diligently treated if it is to be controlled. If tetracycline does not seem to control it, I switch to ampicillin, repeating the treatment after siphoning every other day until four treatments have been made.

The antibiotics in the tetracycline group are known as bacteriostatic antibiotics, meaning that they suppress the growth of, rather than kill outright, the pathogenic organisms they are intended to combat. The bactericidal antibiotics, on the other hand, destroy the pathogenic organisms instead of just controlling their proliferation. In most cases, the faster the pathogenic organisms are growing, the faster a bactericidal antibiotic will work against them. Ampicillin, one of the bactericidal antibiotics, is most effective when combined with formaldehyde at the rate of 2 drops per gallon of water. As with foods, new antibiotics and other forms of remedies for guppy ailments are being introduced to the aquarium market all the time, and it is best to check with your dealer and other experienced guppy hobbyists to find out what is best to use to combat particular diseases.

In recent years incidences of guppies' infestation by crustacean and helminthic parasites have been reported with greater frequency than ever had been the case before. Above is a closeup of the anal area of a female guppy being parasitized by the worm *Camallanus*, an especially debilitating parasite that for a while threatened to wipe out entire guppy strains. The parasite can be effectively controlled by medicating the guppies' food; use 25 milligrams of piperazine for every 10 grams of food. Photo by Dr. Gottfried Schubert.

This albino is what is known among guppy people as a "mule"—it's a female that has changed into a male, the tip-offs being the exceptionally large body and the very small caudal. Photo by Dr. S. Frank.

Red albino bred by Midge Hill. According to the IFGA standards, any guppy having red eyes is classed as an albino. Photo by Midge Hill.

This purple guppy has a major fault: the dorsal is poorly colored in that it is much too light to match the caudal. Uniformity of color between dorsal and caudal is an important judging point according to the standards. Photo by Dr. Herbert R. Axelrod.

Red guppies are very popular on the show circuit, but it is difficult to maintain a strain that consistently shows good size coupled with bright red color. The males with the best red color usually are not the largest males, so it's hard to keep the two traits running in combination. Photo by Dr. Herbert R. Axelrod.

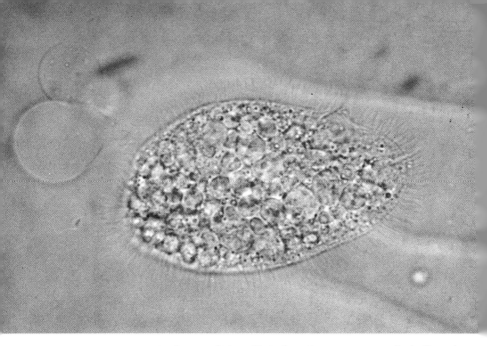

Tetrahymena corlissi, one of the ciliated protozoans generally believed to be responsible for protozoan disease of guppies; another protozoan believed to cause protozoan disease is *Ophryoglena.* Photo by J. Camper.

Split tails are another hazard of showing guppies. As a preventive I add 1 cc of 1000 mcg. water-soluble B-12 into 10 gallons of water. This procedure is repeated every other day during the show life of the guppies. If split tails occur I double and sometimes triple the doses, depending on the severity of the split.

After my show guppies are put into their aquarium and treated with preventive medication (formaldehyde, tetracycline and B-12) they are fed a light feeding of dry food, followed one hour later with live brine shrimp. The next day they go back on my regular feeding program.

Shipping Guppies

When you ship your guppies (and I am assuming that you'll ship them by air), be sure to fill out the airbill completely. Note on special instructions "Hold at Airport. Call on Arrival . . . (and here you give the telephone number of the receiver as listed in the show rules of that particular show).

Have labels already typed up for return shipping and include full instructions as to how you wish your guppies to be handled. In case you are shipping more than one carton, mark cartons "1 of 3", "2 of 3", "3 of 3" (should there be three cartons). Keep an accurate record of the contents of each carton according to number so that should a carton happen to get lost you will be able to tell exactly what is lost, especially for claims purposes.

When selecting flights, allow one or two earlier flights to avoid a late arrival which could mean your fish would not arrive in time to be entered in the show.

PACKING FISH FOR SHIPMENT

Taking the water from the same tank the guppy has been in, I fill a 6" x 10" plastic bag one-quarter full. Then I very carefully put one guppy in this bag. There are several reasons for never putting guppies together in a single bag: guppies nip each other, one might die en route and contaminate the water, etc.

After the guppy is in the bag, inject air, cup the bag, twist its ends, fold down and make secure with a rubber band as tightly as possible. Invert the bag and drop it into a second plastic bag, again twisting,

This is a beautifully colored multicolor guppy, but the dorsal is far too short; a fish like this should not be used as a breeder. Photo by Victor Datzkevich.

This is a beautiful blue delta guppy. Except for the black spot in the small off-color dorsal it would make an excellent breeder. Photo by G. Gellrich.

Gold half-black bred by Ron Yater. Photo by Midge Hill.

folding and securing tightly with a rubber band. Double bagging is very important. A double-bagged guppy stands a better chance of survival than does a single-bagged guppy. Make sure there are no corners in which the guppy can become trapped.

Mark each guppy bag with a waterproof marking pen, giving it a number which coincides with a number on the entry form which gives full information as to the class fish #1 or #2 is to be entered into. For example: #1—class, black delta.

The shipping container should be insulated against temperature changes. Styrofoam® makes a good shipping container. After carefully packing the bags of guppies into the container, include your entry form, entry fees, return shipment information, etc. I seal this information in a plastic bag so that if there is any water leakage the information will remain dry. It's also good to pack extra plastic bags and rubber bands to be used to repack your fish after the show. The insulated shipping container should be sealed all around with tape and placed inside a cardboard container to protect it against any form of rough treatment.

I ship air freight. I don't recommend shipping by mail, as it takes longer and is less reliable. Check well ahead of the shipping date which airline best meets your needs. Most airlines will require the freight to be in their hands at least 1½ hours before departure time. As soon as departure time is confirmed and arrival time is assured, telephone the show representative with the complete information as to airline, flight number, airbill number, date and time of arrival and number of cartons; request a telephone call if any problems arise.

If you are shipping only one or two guppies to a show, air freight is impractical, and you will have to rely on Airmail Special Delivery,

History of the Modern Guppy

by Art Hopkins

In the early 1950's the wide-tail guppy was being developed and exhibited mainly in the eastern part of the country. In 1957 *Tropical Fish Hobbyist* magazine and other publications published a fabulous offer to all aquarium societies in the United States. The offer, made by Larry Konig and Dr. John Rutkowski, was to give a pair of their strain of show guppies to any aquarium society that would form a guppy committee or group within their society. For the first time excellent breeding stock was distributed throughout the United States. In 1961 a very progressive organization of aquarium societies known as the Northeast Council of Aquarium Societies developed the American Guppy Association standards; from there they developed the A.G.A. point system. In a very short time this was the most widely accepted standard and point system for judging guppies in the United States.

In the early 1960's the exhibiting of fancy guppies centered in the Mid-west, mainly in Wisconsin, Illinois, Indiana, and Ohio. In 1964 a group of hobbyists from these states met in Cincinnati, Ohio, to discuss and form an organization to better serve the needs of the midwest area. The purposes were to further the ideas of the American Guppy Association and standardize such things as exhibition bowls, training and qualifying judges, establishing a show schedule, and updating standards.

Ed Hazle of Cuyahoga Falls, Ohio, served as our first chairman until 1966 when the International

The multicolor classes at IFGA shows get many large, colorful males similar to the one shown here, but this fish would be held back because of its comparatively small dorsal. Photo by Victor Datzkevich.

The occurrence of Siamese twins among livebearing fishes and guppies in particular is not extremely rare, and such fish are generally valueless except as curiosities or for scientific experimentation. Photo by Dr. S. Frank.

This half-black blue has good body shape and size and good caudal shape, size and color, but the color of the dorsal is very poor. Photo by Dr. Herbert R. Axelrod.

This purple male has good dorsal shape and length but very poor color in the dorsal. It has other faults as well and serves as a good example of a fish that would be faulted because of the unevenness of its top-line: note the slight hump just to the right of the eye. Photo by Dr. Herbert R. Axelrod.

Two of the older great names among celebrated guppy breeders: left, William Sternke; at right below is Paul Hahnel, probably the most famous guppy breeder of all time. With him is shown the Brazilian ethnologist Harald Schultz. Photo by Dr. Herbert R. Axelrod.

Guppy Breeders of the 1970's: on this page and the following pages you'll find photos of some of the best-known guppy breeders of the 1970's, men who've *proved* that they can produce good guppies by having their guppies shown in competition and winning under trained impartial judges.

Mike Regent,
New Jersey.
Photo by
Alice Regent.

James Pupelis, Illinois.

Foo Phang Ting, Singapore. Photo by Dr. Herbert R. Axelrod.

This half-black red guppy has good body size and very good caudal color; except for its poor dorsal color, it would make a good breeder. Photo by Dr. Herbert R. Axelrod.

A yellow snakeskin—the yellow snakeskin is just one of the many new color varieties that has been developed over the last few years. Photo by Dr. Herbert R. Axelrod.

Although their dorsals need improvement as far as length is concerned, these two matched males are above average snakeskins. They have very good caudal shape and decent caudal and body color. These are young fish; they were bred by Foo Phang Ting in Singapore. Photo by Dr. Herbert R. Axelrod.

Glen Parrish,
California.

Jim Horan,
Illinois.

William Illig,
Ohio.

Stan Shubel,
Michigan (Stan's wife
Ethel is also very well
known among IFGA
exhibitors; she's an
accredited IFGA
judge and was voted
into the Guppy Hall of
Fame in 1976). Photo
by M. McRae.

Dale Marteeny, California. Photo by Midge Hill.

Fancy Guppy Association was formed. Dick Eisenmann served as President for two years. Stan Shubel became President in December, 1968, and served until December, 1972. Art Hopkins of Cincinnati, Ohio, became President in December, 1972, and served until replaced by John Wolcott in 1975.

In the years since its formation the I.F.G.A. has established a judging standard and has done much to regularize all of the rules of organized guppy-showing while helping guppies to reach new heights of popularity. The I.F.G.A. currently has twelve sanctioned shows a year, an annual seminar for judging guppies, and an outstanding monthly publication.

This purple veiltail has one good point (its big body), but its many faults far outweigh that one asset. The caudal is both badly shaped and poor in color, and the dorsal is far too light. Photo by Dr. Herbert R. Axelrod.

This four-month-old male comes from an outstanding strain, its ancestors having won the IFGA World Class championship for half-black AOC for five years in a row (1971 through 1975) and the World Breeder Class championship. Photo by Dr. Herbert R. Axelrod of a fish bred by the author.

Males of the author's strain of half-black pastels have won their World Class championship three years consecutively (1973, 1974, 1975). . . but it required giving them the utmost in good care and absolutely ruthless culling. Photo by Dr. Herbert R. Axelrod.

An albino snakeskin bred by Midge Hill; albino snakeskins are relatively rare on the show circuit. Photo by Midge Hill.

IFGA Competition Classes

Before we get into the presentation of the actual standards for the various different guppy types that are exhibited on the show circuit of the International Fancy Guppy Association, I'll give you a loose review of the structure of IFGA itself, because an understanding of the structure will enable you to better appreciate some of the rules and regulations.

The IFGA rules and regulations make sense. Some of them are so obviously in tune with what guppy breeders need and want that they go unquestioned by anyone, but some of them become the subject of debate among active breeder/exhibitors. Whether the regulations and standards go unchallenged or are fought over, the point to remember is that IFGA is basically an organization that is responsive to the concerns of the people it serves. . . it is not a government lorded over by some dictator type who manages to have his way about everything. Because guppies change and breeders' requirements change, IFGA changes too. The rules and regulations laid down by the organization are written by guppy people for guppy people; when they don't work out, they're thrown out. I'm not going to try to tell you that all of the rules of the IFGA are easily learned in a few minutes of reading time. They're not. They take time to learn, and in order to learn them well you need more than just time: you need plenty of experience as well. It simply isn't enough that you know the words. . . you have to develop the correct feel for what you're doing, and the only way you can develop that feel is to get in there and exhibit, or at least attend the shows.

What I'm presenting here is a very sketchy outline of the rules and regulations, enough to give you some *basic* information. You can easily obtain all of the specific information you want by contacting the IFGA itself. The IFGA publishes a booklet listing all current rules and regulations and all current judging standards applicable at IFGA-sanctioned shows; the current price of the book is $2.00, but of course the price is subject to change from time to time. Since *Tropical Fish Hobbyist* magazine regularly publishes listings of the names and addresses of individuals whom you can contact to obtain information about the IFGA and other national specialty clubs, refer to current issues of *Tropical Fish Hobbyist* for up-to-date listings.

The IFGA is not composed of a membership of individuals. Instead, it is composed of a group of member guppy *clubs*. You as an individual don't become a member of IFGA; you as an individual become a member of a guppy specialty club that is a member of IFGA. Currently there are 43 such IFGA-affiliated guppy clubs.

One of the most important functions IFGA performs for the guppy fancy is to serve as the clearinghouse and arbiter of show rules for all IFGA-sanctioned shows. The importance of this function, of course, is that it allows guppy exhibitors to compete on a uniform basis. The rules for each show are the same in all significant respects, so you don't run into situations in which somebody keeps rewriting the rules from show to show. You can have variation in unimportant details, but you don't have a case in which you get all set to ship your fish to the show and then discover that males are going to be judged

This fish has good red color in the caudal, but the black spots in the same fin mark it as a loser as a breeder. Photo by Dr. Herbert R. Axelrod.

This four-month-old blue delta has one major (dorsal too light) and one minor (body could be a little bigger) fault, but representatives of its strain have won a World Blue Class championship and a number of best in shows. Photo by Dr. Herbert R. Axelrod of fish bred by the author.

This purple veiltail illustrates two faults that any serious guppy breeder should be on the lookout for when selecting breeding stock. The fish has an off-color dorsal fin, and it also has a concave outline between the eye and the dorsal. Photo by Dr. Herbert R. Axelrod.

A half-black bicolor bred by Glen Parrish. Photo by Midge Hill.

according to how well they resemble neon tetras and that only females that have produced at least 100 young each are the only ones that can be shown. If it's an IFGA-sanctioned show, you'll have no curve balls thrown at you. . . each show will be basically the same as the one that preceded it on the circuit, regardless of where it's held, Maumee Valley or Puerto Rico, Sacramento or Singapore.

Another very important contribution made to the guppy fancy by the IFGA is the uniformity of the judging standards. There currently are 35 judges accredited by the IFGA, and all of the judges know their guppies. They've got good practical experience, and they've been able to pass all the stiff tests administered to IFGA judging applicants.

POINT SHOWS

IFGA sanctions two types of shows. First there are the **point shows**, and they're called point shows because they're the only ones at which you can win points that put you in the running for the annual IFGA championship awards. There are a number of championship awards given out, and the way that you win the awards is to compile the most points in the award categories. Suppose you have a good strain of half-black blues, for example; if during a given show season you win enough points with them at IFGA point shows, you can become the IFGA World Champion breeder of half-black blue guppies for that season. It is easy to figure out how many points toward championship a win at any given show will provide for you: you take the actual number of points won at the show in the class in which you're competing and multiply that number by the weight-number of the show. The weight number of the show is assigned by IFGA according to the num-

Chris McKay of Ontario, Canada poses with just a part of his guppy trophy collection. If you have good guppies and want to assemble an impressive collection of memorabilia, guppy shows offer a fun-filled way to do it. . . but remember that it's not easy, because the competition is stiff.

ber of classes at the show; the more classes, the higher the weight-number. A show having 40 to 49 classes is a 4-point show; a show having 50 to 59 classes is a 5-point show; a show having 60 to 69 classes is a 6-point show, and a show having 70 to 79 classes is a 7-point show. Therefore if you score a first-place win (worth ten points) with your half-black blues at an IFGA-sanctioned show having 54 competition classes, you will have earned 50 points toward championship in the half-black blue class. If you score a second place win (worth 8 points) at a show having 72 competition classes, you will have

Female guppies, once so drab and unattractive that they were seldom even looked at, now command attention for their own interesting colors and color patterns. Shown at left is a half-black blue; below is a red bred by Bruce Carter. Photo of blue female by Dr. W. Foersch; photo of red female by Midge Hill.

Two interesting female guppies from Europe. The fish above (photo by Victor Datzkevich) shows good size to her caudal and a nice carry-over of pattern from dorsal to caudal; the lower female (photo by Dr. S. Frank) is an exceptional half-black female showing large body and caudal and a very fine match between dorsal and caudal.

earned 56 points toward the half-black blue championship. A third-place win in a color class calling for the entry of a single fish is worth 6 points, and a fourth-place win is worth 4 points, incidentally. There are five other basic point arrangements for wins (breeder class, males: 50 points for first place, 40 for second place, 30 points for third place, 20 points for fourth place; breeder class, females: 30, 24, 18 and 12 points for first through fourth place wins, respectively; best in show, single fish: 25, 20, 15 and 10 points respectively; tank entries: 20, 16, 12 and 8 points respectively; best in show, tanks: 50, 40, 30 and 20 points respectively.) No matter how many points are won in a particular class, the IFGA championship points are figured by multiplying the number of basic show points by the number-weight of the show. In addition to the championships awarded in the color classes, the IFGA also presents championship trophies for breeder champion classes in both male and female categories and for grand over-all male and grand over-all female; grand over-all male is in my opinion the most important championship in the field.

You can see that the way the championship points are figured tends to make the bigger shows—that is, the ones having more competition classes—more valuable as contributors to your point score. The bigger shows therefore become more attractive to exhibitors, especially the exhibitors who are in the running for championships. The bigger shows therefore generally provide a stiffer degree of competition, since you have both more and somewhat better entries to compete against. In other words, the bigger shows give you more points but are harder to win at—which is exactly the way it should be.

Each year the IFGA publishes a list of the point shows scheduled to be held during the show season which runs from April through October; there were twelve point shows scheduled for the 1976 show season. Point shows are sponsored by the member clubs on a rotating basis, and each year one member club is chosen as host club for the annual show/ convention, which is held in November.

NON-POINT SHOWS

Non-point shows sanctioned by IFGA can be held even by guppy clubs that are not IFGA member clubs, but of course in all such cases the IFGA show rules and standards have to apply, and an IFGA judge must be at the show. IFGA-sanctioned non-point shows can have as many classes as the point shows have, but the classes must include the following ten: red, blue, green, black, half-black, multicolor, snakeskin, any other color, females and matched males (two).

In addition to being guppy shows and therefore enjoyable by guppy fanciers even though there are no championship points involved, the non-point shows also offer guppy exhibitors opportunities to gain experience. Exhibitors aren't the only ones to gain valuable experience at the non-point shows, either, because the non-point shows also provide the place where potential IFGA judges get their judging experience. There is no limit to the number of non-point IFGA-sanctioned guppy shows that can be held each year.

IFGA COMPETITION CLASSES

There are 26 separate classifications under which points may be accumulated by exhibitors of guppies to qualify for championships awarded by

This green bicolor's best days are behind it, but it once must have been an excellent fish. It has a large caudal and beautiful dorsal, and its body shape is near perfect. Except for its ragged tail—which almost certainly is the result of old age—it would be a leading contender for best in show. Photo by H. Hansen, Aquarium Berlin.

Purple snakeskin bred by the author; the purple snakeskin is a comparatively new color variety on the show circuit. Photo by Dr. Herbert R. Axelrod.

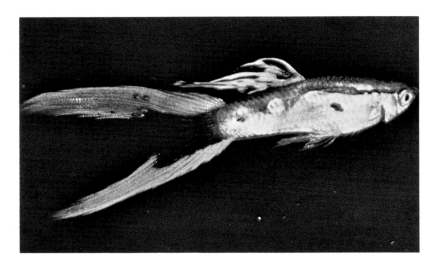

Swordtail guppies are not currently among the most popular varieties at the big guppy shows, but they have a dedicated core of breeders and fanciers. This double-sword was bred by W. and D. Reynolds.

A strain of snakeskin guppies from Singapore. Photo by Midge Hill.

the International Fancy Guppy Association. Naturally, since there is a much greater variation in body color and tail color and other secondary sexual characteristics among male guppies than there is among female guppies, there have to be more classifications under which males are judged, and there are. Nineteen of the 26 classifications are for males.

The 26 classifications are basic classifications—that is, they are intended to be mutually exclusive, so that any given fish can't be placed into more than one class at the same time. There are many variations on the basic classifications, so most IFGA-sanctioned guppy shows have many more than 26 basic classes in which guppies may compete for points, but regardless of how many show classes there are, points can be accumulated in only the basic 26 categories.

Male Classes

Of the nineteen basic classifications in which male guppies may be shown, eighteen classifications are determined according to the physical appearance (especially the color of body and tail) of the fish themselves, and one class is determined according to the number of fish entered. This latter class is called the "breeder" class and consists of an entry of five males that will be judged primarily according to how well they match each other in looks. . . that is, their uniformity of appearance.

CLASSES BY BODY COLOR:

There are two classifications that are determined by body color alone: gold class and bronze class.

GOLD: a gold guppy is one having a butter-yellow body overlaid with a pinkish cast.

BRONZE: a bronze guppy has a dark golden

body on which each scale is outlined in black.

CLASSES BY COLOR PATTERN ON THE BODY:
There is one classification that is determined by the pattern of color on the body; this is the *SNAKE-SKIN* class.

In order to qualify as a snakeskin, a guppy has to have a distinctly vermiculated pattern over its entire body. The snakeskin pattern can be formed by two different colors or by varying shades of the same color, but the pattern of vermiculations must

Snakeskins are popular on the guppy show circuit. Guppies referred to as "cobra" guppies are fish having vertical bars along their sides in what guppy geneticists refer to as the "zebrinous" pattern, but such fish are not classed as snakeskin guppies for IFGA show purposes; a snakeskin guppy must have the vermiculated pattern. Photo by Dr. Herbert R. Axelrod.

be present. The words used by the IFGA to describe the snakeskin pattern are "chain-link or rosette pattern." The snakeskin pattern is hard to describe but easy to recognize once you've seen a good example of the class.

At shows, snakeskins are usually split into two

This snakeskin male would not make a good breeder, because it has bad qualities (skinny body, unmatched caudal and dorsal color, bad dorsal color) that probably would be transmitted to its offspring. Photo by Dr. Herbert R. Axelrod.

This bicolor guppy has excellent color in its caudal fin, but its dorsal fin is poor in both color and size. Photo by Victor Datzkevitch.

Yellow guppies seen on the show circuit are usually small, poorly colored fish, but this one is a winner. It has a large caudal, large body and a nicely matching dorsal. Photo by Midge Hifl of fish bred by Stan Shubel, IFGA Yellow Class champion in 1971.

Blue snakeskin bred by Dale Marteeny. Photo by Midge Hill.

color groupings. Solid-color snakeskins make up one group, and variegated snakeskins make up the other.

CLASSES BY EYE COLOR:

Only one classification is made according to the eye color of the fish. This is the ALBINO class. Any guppy that has red or pink eyes is classed as an albino no matter what the color of its body or tail.

CLASSES BY TAIL TYPE:

One class is reserved for SWORDTAIL guppies. In order to qualify as a swordtail, a guppy has to have a recognizable extension to its caudal fin. The extension can be on the bottom of the fin only, on the top of the fin only or on both the bottom and top of the fin. (European guppy shows split swordtail guppies into top-sword, bottom-sword and top-and-bottom-sword classes, but American shows do not.)

Swordtail guppies. Photo by Mervin F. Roberts.

CLASSES BY COMBINATION OF BODY COLOR AND TAIL COLOR:

The HALF-BLACK guppies are the only ones in which both body color and tail color combine to determine the show classification of the fish. A half-black guppy is colored black (the black can and of course does vary in intensity, but it must be recognizably in the black range) from the ventral fins back to the caudal peduncle. The fish can have a *greater* extent of black on its body (from the caudal peduncle forward to right behind the eyes, for example) and still qualify as a half-black, but it can't have a lesser extent and still qualify as a half-black. There are many three-quarters black guppies, for example. There is a little confusion here, because not every half-black guppy is categorized for show purposes in the half-black classes. One type of half-black guppy is classed according to its tail color, not by a combination of its tail and body color. That one exception is the half-black guppy that has a black tail. A fish with a half-black body and a black tail is categorized according to its tail color alone and is judged with the fish that are grouped according to tail color; it is taken out of the half-black classes and judged in the black class of the tail-color classes.

The four color classes set up for half-black guppies are: half-black red, half-black blue, half-black pastel and half-black any other color (AOC). Pastel is defined by the IFGA as being a light shade of any basic color, and any other color is any color other than those covered by the classes set up for half-blacks.

CLASSES BY TAIL COLOR:

There are nine color classes that are determined by the color of the tail of the fish. These nine

Girardinus metallicus, tribe Girardinini. Photo by H. Hansen, Aquarium Berlin.

Phalloceros caudomaculatus, tribe Cnesterodontini. Photo by R. Zukal.

Gambusia affinis, tribe Gambusinini. Photo by R. Zukal.

The current taxonomic placement of the guppy (according to the most recent generally accepted revision, that of 1963 by Drs. Donn Eric Rosen and Reeve M. Bailey) classifies the guppy as *Poecilia reticulata*, a member of the family of livebearing fishes known collectively as the Poeciliidae within the order Cyprinodontiformes. (The guppy until that time was known most usually under the name *Lebistes reticulatus*, and some current opinion still retains the generic designation *Lebistes* as the subgeneric taxon for *Poecilia reticulata*.) As a member of the genus *Poecilia*, the guppy is closely related to a number of other popular livebearers (the mollies and limias, for example, both of which are also now considered to be within the genus *Poecilia*.) Oddly enough, some of the livebearing species that look most like guppies are not as closely related to guppies as some less similar-looking livebearers are. *Gambusia* species, for instance, are less closely related to the guppy than swordtails are, because they are placed in a different tribe—yet even an experienced hobbyist would have great difficulty in distinguishing a wild female *Gambusia affinis* from a wild female guppy, whereas he'd have no trouble identifying a female swordtail in distinction to a female guppy.

classes are: red, blue, green, black, purple, yellow, any other color, multicolor and bicolor.

A *bicolor*-tail guppy is one in which the tail has two different basic colors, and the secondary color must make up at least 25% of the color in the tail. A *multicolor*-tail guppy is one in which there are more than two basic colors in the tail.

Female Classes

There are seven basic show categories for female guppies. As with the males, body color, tail color and a combination of body color and tail color play a part in determining the show classification into which female guppies fit.

The seven show classes for female guppies are:

HALF-BLACK—having a body color the same as described for male half-black guppy. The same restriction applies to half-black females having a black tail as applies to half-black males having a black tail: such fish are shown in the black class, not the half-black class.

GOLD—having a body color as described for a male gold guppy.

BLACK—having a black tail.

BLUE/GREEN—having a blue or green tail.

RED—having a red tail.

ANY OTHER COLOR—having a tail any color other than red, blue, green or black.

BREEDER—This class is for an entry of three matched females, regardless of body or tail color.

Variations on the Basic Classes

Most of the 19 basic male classes can be further subdivided into many more classes by taking into account the shape of the tail (that is, whether it's a veil tail or a delta tail) and by setting up another classification for what is called the "tank" class (a "tank" being defined as two matched fish). Therefore a basic class like snakeskin can be turned into a delta snakeskin class and a veil snakeskin class and a tank snakeskin class, and most of the other basic classes can be given the same treatment. The only ones that can't are the ones that are mutually exclusive; you couldn't, for example, have a breeder tank class.

The practical result of all this subdivisioning of the basic classes is to create many more than 26 classes in which fish can be exhibited at the guppy shows, and that's exactly what is done. Guppy shows currently are averaging about seventy exhibit classes at each show.

SOME REMARKS ON SHOW CLASSIFICATIONS

As I mentioned in the beginning of this section, the show classifications currently applying to guppy shows are intended to be mutually exclusive so that a guppy cannot logically be placed into two or more classifications at the same time. Unfortunately, because of the multiplicity of colors and color patterns that can be found among guppies and because people—including the people who set up the show classifications for guppies—differ in their opinions about colors and shapes and just about everything else, it doesn't always work out that way, and sometimes there is a lot of confusion over which categorizing factor takes precedence over another categorizing factor. Suppose, for example, you had an albino guppy that showed the swordtail tail characteristic. Where would it go in a show, in the albino class or the swordtail class? Or suppose you had a half-black swordtail. Would it be classed as a half-black, or would it be classed as a swordtail? And

A half-black red with poorly colored caudal and dorsal and very little uniformity of color. Photo by H. Hansen, Aquarium Berlin.

Anyone who breeds fish like this to exhibit on the fancy guppy show circuit is wasting his time. It's not a question of taste—anyone who prefers plain guppies over fancy guppies is entirely free to do so—but he'd better do it with the understanding that they just don't live up to show standards and therefore are never going to win any prizes. Photo by R. Zukal.

what would be the reasoning behind its classification, regardless of the outcome? Before you can get a good grip on what the show classifications mean and how they are applied, you have to get some experience in what the guppy shows and guppy people are like, what they consider of prime importance and what they consider of secondary importance. In other words, you have to get some good firsthand experience. The only practical way for you to get that experience is to go to the shows. You don't have to exhibit fish yourself, but you do have to attend. You have to be there and look and listen and learn. Believe me, there is no better, faster, sure way to learn about the mechanics of guppy shows than to attend them as regularly as you can. If you do attend, you'll learn a lot more than just how guppy shows are run, too—you'll also learn much about how to feed and raise and breed guppies. This is because, first of all, the exhibitors at guppy shows and the people who attend guppy shows regularly are the most knowledgeable guppy people in the world; they as a group know more about raising *good* guppies than anyone else does. Additionally, they're not stingy with their information. They give good advice and plenty of it, and they don't look down their noses at the people who ask them for it. Maybe they remember when they were in the same position of having to look for good advice, maybe they're just extra-nice people, maybe they think they have something to gain. . . I don't know. I just know that they're among the finest people in the aquarium hobby.

I also know that the competition at guppy shows is getting keener all the time. When I first started on the show circuit there was just a handful of outstanding guppy breeders, people like Chris McKay of Toronto, Canada with his blues; Mike Shye of Missouri with his half-black reds; Dale Marteeny of California with his bicolors and snakeskins; Stan Shubel of Michigan with his golds and yellows and blues. Then the following breeders came onto the scene and did very well: Dave LeValley of Ohio with multis; Bill Illig (Ohio) with yellow and blue snakeskins; Dave Crabtree (Ohio), multis; Ron Yater (Indiana), half-black pastels; Harold Morgan (Texas), reds; Joe Rack (Montreal, Canada), bicolors; Jim Pupelis (Illinois), blues; Rich Szydlk (Illinois), beautiful big females. . . and now we have Jim Horan (Illinois) with multis, snakeskins, and swordtails, and Glen Parrish (California) with exceptionally large blues, greens, and purples. From a mere handful of good breeders that any one show used to be able to represent, today there are fifteen or twenty outstanding guppy breeders who can beat you at any given show.

IFGA *Judging Standards*

In this section I'm going to cover the standards by which IFGA judges select winning guppies in each class. While you're reading this section, please keep two things in mind. The first thing to remember is that these standards have been set up by the IFGA to provide criteria against which each fish may be judged. . . the fish described in the standards have been determined to be perfect models that breeders can try to match as closely as possible. The fish described in the standards don't really exist. . . some real fish may come close to matching them, but no real fish can *completely* match the perfection described in the standards. The second thing to remember is that the standards as given here are *my* words, not the official standards as published by the IFGA. I mention this because I have to admit that I am nowhere near being an expert interpreter of the standards, and some of the things in the standards are a real puzzle to me. For example, the standards for the veil, delta and super widetail guppies seem to me to be written in such a way that some very good guppies would not fit into any classification. The standard for the veiltail guppy, for instance, says that a tail spread of 45 degrees is ideal within an acceptable range of 40 to 50 degrees, and the standard for the deltatail guppy says that a spread of 60 degrees is ideal within an acceptable range of 55 to 65 degrees, and the standard for the super widetail guppy says that a spread of 90 degrees is ideal, with 70 degrees of spread being the minimum acceptable spread. Then what happens to guppies having spreads between 50 and 55 degrees or 65 to 70 degrees? In practical application at the shows, of course, they are placed into one group or another, but such placements are not strictly according to the standards. I'm just pointing out that I'm not an accredited IFGA judge and that I'm not up on all of the fine points—there are many—of judging guppies. If you want absolutely definitive pronouncements about the exact wording of the standards and what they mean, you'll just have to get them from the IFGA.

You'll notice that the standards fall into five main sections, with a separate standard for veiltail, deltatail, super widetail swordtail and female guppies. Each standard provides a description of what the body, dorsal fin, caudal fin and color of the fish *should* be. As far as color is concerned where it is described in the standards, uniformity of color is currently what is being called for. The colors of the fins should match the color of the body and, where two colors are involved, two different shades of the same basic color are preferred to two different colors. You can disagree with the desirability of this policy if you want to, but that's the way it is: uniformity is what the standard calls for, and on that basis the fish that show the greatest degree of uniformity in a given competition class are the ones that are going to win the awards. Brightness of color is second to uniformity of color in importance, but it is important; uniformly vivid colors are much preferred over uniformly drab colors. Another thread of uniformity that runs through all of the standards is concerned with body outline. The standard for all guppies calls for a well-rounded body and decries a body that is humped or one that has a nicely rounded body onto which is attached a flat head. In other words, all guppies should have a regular and not too steep outline to their bodies, and there are to be no pronounced high spots or flat spots. This holds true for veiltails, deltatails, super widetails, swordtails and females.

Point values have been assigned to the size, shape, color and condition of a guppy's dorsal and tail fin as well as its body, and two other features, deportment (that is, the fish's general behavior, the way it holds itself) and symmetry (the way each feature blends into a harmonious whole) also have been assigned point values. The different features have different point values in the judging of male and female guppies, naturally. Here are the current point scales:

Point scale for judging male guppies:

Body size, 10 points; body color, 8 points; body shape, 4 points; body condition, 3 points. Total body points: 25.

Dorsal fin size, 10 points; dorsal fin color, 8 points; dorsal fin shape, 4 points; dorsal fin condition, 3 points. Total dorsal points: 25.

Caudal fin size, 13 points; caudal fin color, 12 points; caudal fin shape, 10 points; caudal fin condition, 5 points. Total caudal points: 40.

Deportment: 5 points.

Symmetry: 5 points.

Point scale for judging female guppies:

Body size, 13 points; body color, 5 points; body shape, 9 points; body condition, 3 points. Total body points: 30.

Dorsal fin size, 7 points; dorsal fin color, 6 points; dorsal fin shape, 4 points; dorsal fin condition, 3 points. Total dorsal points: 20

Caudal fin size, 13 points; caudal fin color, 12 points; caudal fin shape, 10 points; caudal fin condition, 5 points. Total caudal points: 40.

Deportment: 5 points.

Symmetry: 5 points.

The above point values and totals are for fish judged as individuals; for entries in the tank and breeder classes, 10 points per fish can be added for similarity. (Two matched males constitute a *tank* entry; five matched males constitute an entry in the breeder male class; three matched females constitute an entry in the breeder female class.) The point values and totals are *maximum* values... no matter how good a fish's tail is, it can't earn its owner any more than 40 points. On the deduction side, up to 10 points may be deducted for a body deformity. (The currently most seriously penalized body deformity is a clipped gonopodium, which causes the maximum 10-point penalization.) In addition to being penalized, fish can be disqualified entirely if they are entered into the wrong class for color or tail shape or if they are just plain too runty or otherwise bad. Incidentally, you can't show a dead fish no matter how good it is, because Rule #3, Section III (Entries) of the IFGA show rules says that a fish has to be alive to be judged. Another thing you can't show is somebody else's fish; Rule #1 of the section cited above demands that the fish you show be born in your tanks and raised in your tanks.

Standard for the veiltail guppy:

BODY: The body of a veiltail guppy should be as long as the tail, and the caudal peduncle should be 1½ times as long as it is high. The caudal peduncle should look (and, of course, be) strong enough to carry the tail.

DORSAL FIN: The dorsal fin of a veiltail guppy should be in the form of a parallelogram the long sides (the fin's length) of which are at least four times as long as its short sides (the fin's height , not counting its point of attachment at the guppy's back). The dorsal fin should be held erect and should be straight.

CAUDAL FIN: The tail fin of a veiltail guppy should spread out from the caudal peduncle at an angle of 45 degrees to form an isosceles triangle; a spread of 40 to 50 degrees is acceptable. Since an angle of 45 degrees is ideal at the peduncle, angles of 67½ degrees are ideal at the rearmost corners of the fin. The rear edge of the fin should

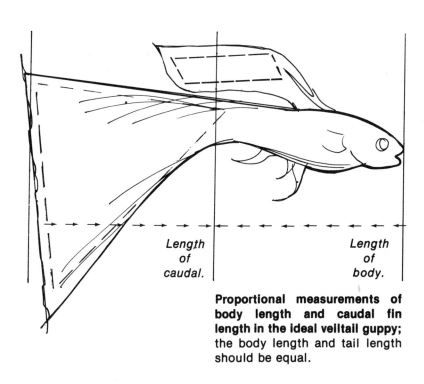

Length of caudal.

Length of body.

Proportional measurements of body length and caudal fin length in the ideal veiltail guppy; the body length and tail length should be equal.

be even or very slightly indented, and if it is indented slightly the indentations should be regular, not erratic; the rearmost edge of the fin should not be heavily indented or frayed, and the fin should be carried erect and spread wide.

Standard for the deltatail guppy:

BODY: The body of a deltatail guppy should be as long as the fish's tail. The caudal peduncle should be 1½ times as long as it is high, and regardless of its exact proportion it should look strong enough to support the tail fin.

DORSAL FIN: The dorsal fin of a deltatail guppy should be in the form of a parallelogram, with the long sides of the parallelogram (the fin's length) being three times as long as the short sides of the parallelogram (the fin's height, not counting its point of attachment at the guppy's back). The dorsal should be held erect.

CAUDAL FIN: The tail fin of a deltatail guppy should be in the shape of a equilateral triangle

Proportional measurements of body length and caudal fin length in the ideal deltatail guppy; the body length and caudal length should be equal:

Length of body.

Length of caudal.

Dorsal and caudal fin proportions of the ideal deltatail guppy; a parallelogram having a length three times its height is superimposed over the dorsal fin, and an equilateral triangle is superimposed over the caudal fin and caudal peduncle.

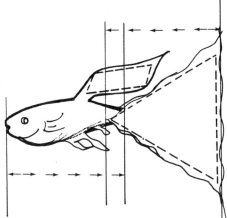

(all three sides equal in length) spreading outward from the fish's caudal peduncle. Since all angles in an equilateral triangle have to be 60 degrees, 60 degrees is the ideal for each angle in the imaginary equilaterally triangular tail of a deltatail guppy. Anything between 55 and 65 degrees is acceptable, but 60 degrees is ideal. The rear edge of the fin should be even; it can be fringed, but it shouldn't be heavily indented or frayed. The fin should be carried erect and spread wide.

Standard for the super widetail guppy:

BODY: The standard calls for the same type of body for a super widetail guppy as for a veiltail or deltatail guppy: the body should be as long as the tail, and the caudal peduncle should be 1½ times as long as it is high.

DORSAL FIN: The dorsal fin of a super widetail guppy should be in the form of a parallelogram, with the long sides of the parallelogram (the fin's length) being three times as long as the short sides of the parallelogram (the fin's height, not counting its point of attachment at the guppy's back).

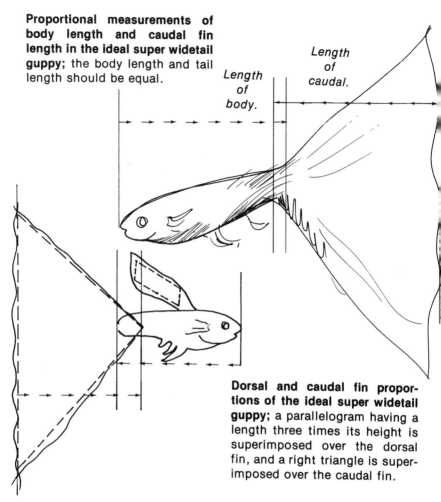

Proportional measurements of body length and caudal fin length in the ideal super widetail guppy; the body length and tail length should be equal.

Length of body.

Length of caudal.

Dorsal and caudal fin proportions of the ideal super widetail guppy; a parallelogram having a length three times its height is superimposed over the dorsal fin, and a right triangle is superimposed over the caudal fin.

CAUDAL FIN: The tail fin of a super widetail guppy should be in the form of a right triangle, with the right angle of the triangle being formed by the edges of the fin as it spreads out from the body. Since a 90-degree angle is the ideal spread of the angle formed by the junction of body and tail, 45 degrees is the ideal spread for the other angles in the tail. An angle of 70 degrees at the junction of peduncle and tail is considered acceptable, and angles of over 90 degrees at the same spot will not be penalized if they don't affect the desired 1:1 ratio of body to tail, so you can see that there can be a large variation in tail shape among super widetail guppies. Just remember that the standard expresses a right angle as the ideal; a widely obtuse angle might be quite an achievement for a breeder, but it's not in accordance with the standard of perfection.

Standard for the swordtail guppy:

BODY: The body of a swordtail guppy should be as long as the fish's tail. The caudal peduncle should be 1½ times as long as it is high and strong enough to carry the tail.

DORSAL FIN: The dorsal fin of a swordtail guppy should be five times as long as its height (not counting the point of attachment at the fish's back); the dorsal fin should extend back a good distance past the caudal peduncle.

CAUDAL FIN: Whether the swordtail guppy being exhibited is a top-sword or bottom-sword, the "sword" part of the tail should look like a sword. It shouldn't look like a banana or rifle or half of a

Proportional measurements of body length and caudal fin length in the ideal swordtail guppy; the body length and tail length should be equal.

Length of body.

Length of caudal.

Dorsal fin proportions of the ideal swordtail guppy; a parallelogram having a length five times its height is superimposed over the dorsal fin.

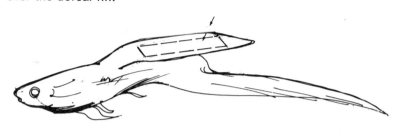

ragged flag. . . it should look like a sword. This means that it should taper to a point at its end, and an even taper is better than an abrupt taper (although even an abrupt taper is better than no taper at all). In a double-sword guppy, each of the swords should be of equal length, and each should be in the same form as for a top-sword or bottom-sword guppy.

Standard for female guppies:

BODY: The body of a female guppy should be three times as long as the fish's tail, and the fish should show good over-all symmetry. The caudal peduncle should be obviously strong enough to carry the tail. A female guppy should have a nicely rounded anal fin and must show a gravid spot.

DORSAL FIN: The dorsal fin should be in proportion to the size of the tail fin so as to preserve over-all symmetry and balance. If a female has a large caudal she should also have a large dorsal, and if the caudal is small the dorsal should be small. Balance is more important than the sheer size of either fin.

Proportional measurements of body length and caudal fin length in three ideal female guppies having different tail shapes; the body should be three times as long as the tail.

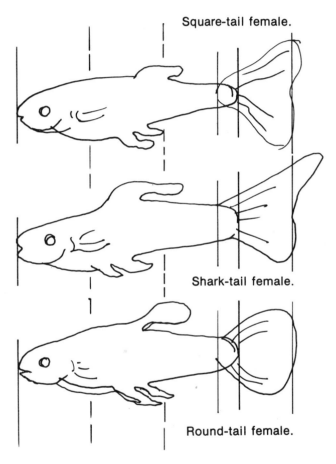

Square-tail female.

Shark-tail female.

Round-tail female.

CAUDAL FIN: The rearmost edge of the tail fin should be even, not indented or frayed, and the tail fin should be kept well spread and not droop-ing. The dorsal fin should be well matched to the caudal fin in color.

Summary

To get a good show fish it is important to start with a guaranteed strain of good guppies from a reputable source, preferably a male and two females. Do not hesitate to pay a premium price to ensure that you get what you really want.

A fancier working with only one strain can do quite well with just six or eight tanks. Tanks of from ten to twenty gallons in capacity are best, as they do not inhibit the growth of the guppies and do not waste space by being larger than is really needed.

For breeding a temperature between 74 and 78 degrees is best. The young fish do best at about 82 degrees for the first few weeks of life, after which the temperature may be lowered towards 76 degrees.

The biggest reason that many fanciers fail to raise guppies to their best is because they do not feed often enough. The time interval between when their digestive tract fills and empties is short. Any healthy guppy will eat ten times a day. I feed live baby brine shrimp twice a day and a variety of dry foods seven times a day. For those who work all day I strongly recommend paste food and live baby brine shrimp, both of which remain in the aquarium for quite some time, enabling the guppies to go on eating throughout the day.

Young guppies that are fed early with live brine shrimp show a tremendous difference in growth and eventual development over those fed predominantly dry food diets.

Everything will go wrong if males and females are left together to breed at random. The quicker, smaller, runty males will do most of the fertilizing. This will cause even the finest of strains to go downhill rapidly. Separate the sexes as soon as possible. At about three weeks it is possible to see a dark spot near the vent in females; males lack this spot. This spot is easier to see if a 100-watt light is held over the babies.

Use only the best young males for breeding. Do not wait until the males are fully matured, as fully developed males are not always fertile or able to catch the females and mate efficiently.

Females can be bred at about two months if they have been properly raised and fed. This lengthens their useful production period because females begin to decline in fertility after the age of about eight to ten months. It is better to breed the selected young guppies in small communities rather than in individual pairs or in large communities. Two males plus five females in a ten-gallon tank is a very good breeding nucleus.

There is no more positive proof of the quality of your guppy stock than to enter them in show competition. . . and no greater satisfaction to be derived from raising show guppies than to win with them consistently.

SUBJECT INDEX